ENDORSEMENTS

"In these pages, Brenda weaves sorrow and hope into a tapestry of living faith. Her testimony reminds us that God's grace transforms even our deepest wounds into a call to love and serve. A moving witness to the power of prayer, perseverance, and the providence of our Heavenly Father."

—Deacon Bob Quinnett,
Blessed Sacrament Catholic Church

"I have known Brenda in my aspects of my life, as a Mayor, Pastor, and friend for many years. Until I read her book, I did not know her full story. I knew her heart for her family, soldiers, and her community, but I did not know how her heart had been broken as a young child and even into motherhood. It would have been easy for Brenda to close her heart to the needs of others since her heart had suffered so much loss, but instead, it expanded the chambers of her heart to help so many others. While Brenda could be enjoying retirement, she has undertaken new roles as a businesswoman, but more important as an advocate for the homeless. I have been in C. Carter Crane and witnessed her immense love for not just a building but the stories that walk through that building week after week. Brenda is driven to be the hands and feet of Jesus to an often forgotten segment of society. I challenge anyone to read the story of a woman who could be broken, but instead is intent on taking the broken and making them whole. I hope this book will propel us all to see people who are broken in a different light, to see them as Jesus saw them, and I really hope it moves us all to action."

—Pastor Larry Thoma,
Elgin First Assembly

"If you are serious about living your best life, living out God's will for your life, then this devotional is for you. Brenda has carefully chosen Scripture verses to provide you purpose, passion, prayerful thought, inspiration, hope, clarity, courage, and conviction. Her use of impactful stories that complement God's Word only enhances the reader's devotional experience. If you want more out of your life, then I highly recommend you not only read this book, but incorporate it into your quiet time and prayer time."

—Jim Fischetti,
President of Brokerage Operations, NextHome.

FAITH
Woven

With Hope and Conviction

BRENDA SPENCER-RAGLAND, Ed.D

LUCIDBOOKS

Faith Woven With Hope and Conviction

Published by Lucid Books in Houston, TX
www.LucidBooks.com

ISBN: 978-1-63296-937-8
eISBN: 978-1-63296-938-5

Special Sales: Most Lucid Books titles are available in special quantity discounts. Custom imprinting or excerpting can also be done to fit special needs. Contact Lucid Books at Info@ LucidBooks.com

*All praise and glory to God,
and appreciation to my family and friends
for their faithful support and encouragement.*

Contents

Reflections of Life

When you're a young girl, and the echoes of your childhood are shaped by domestic violence, life quickly becomes a world of fear and uncertainty. The day your father arrives only to leave you fatherless by its end is a day that redefines everything you know. Not long after, when the walls of your home are consumed by fire, it feels as though the ground beneath you has disappeared entirely. You retreat into silence, scared to speak, unsure of how to navigate a world that feels so broken.

The nights are the hardest. Nightmares haunt you, and the fear of closing your eyes becomes unbearable. Tears stain your pillow as you cry yourself to sleep, dreading the darkness and the terrors it will bring. But even in that darkness, you discover something profound. You learn to pray. Not just as a ritual, but as a lifeline.

With hands clasped tightly, your voice whispers the words, "Now I lay me down to sleep. I pray the Lord my soul to keep. If I should die before I wake, I pray the Lord my soul to take." These words are not just a prayer—they're a shield, a promise, a spark of hope in the midst of the storm. You recite them with unwavering faith, placing your trust in God because He feels like the only one who can quiet the fear that has settled deep inside you.

That simple prayer becomes your strength. It is what carries you through the nights when the nightmares won't relent. It becomes the courage you hold onto in a world that feels unpredictable. And somewhere in the depths of that faith, you begin to find yourself again—not just a scared little girl, but someone who can face the dark with resilience, because you know that even in your darkest moments, you are not alone.

This is not just a story of survival—it's a story of finding faith in the face of fear, and the courage to keep moving forward when the world feels like it's falling apart. Let it inspire you to believe that even in the hardest times, hope can be found, and faith can light the way.

Isaiah 41:10

"Fear not, for I am with you; be not dismayed, for I am your God. I will strengthen you, I will help you, I will uphold you with my righteous right hand."

A Life Forever Changed, and Forever Shaped by Faith

In April 1969, as a young child, my world changed forever in ways I could never have imagined. My father and mother had been arguing—a memory still etched faintly in my mind—and that day, my father was tragically killed. In an instant, my mother became a young widow with eight children to care for.

As if that devastating loss wasn't enough, just two weeks later, another tragedy struck. Our home was completely destroyed in a fire. The memory of that day is hazy but unforgettable. My brother, Jack, and I, young and innocent, had accidentally started the fire. I remember Jack lifting me up so we could grab clothes from the closet, a small candle in hand to light the way. The next thing I knew, the flames had engulfed the clothes and quickly spread.

There are only fragments of memory from those days, but some moments are clear. I remember running to the fence to see my dad and wrapping my small arms around his leg for the last time. I also remember the overwhelming fear as the fire consumed our home, leaving nothing behind but ashes.

Through it all, one truth stands out: God's protection. Though we faced unimaginable loss, my mom and her children were spared—on both occasions. Looking back now, I see His hand, keeping us safe amidst the chaos and tragedy. Even in the darkest moments, His mercy surrounded us and gave us the strength to carry on.

Psalm 46:1-2

"God is our refuge and strength, an ever-present help in trouble. Therefore, we will not fear, though the earth give way and the mountains fall into the heart of the sea."

Unshaken: A Mother's Faith Through the Fire

My mom, a widow with eight children, faced unimaginable trials when her home was destroyed by fire, leaving her and her family homeless. Despite the devastation, she remained resilient, though it often felt like the world was against her—even those she once trusted.

In her struggle to rebuild their lives, she found refuge in an old, forgotten house. There, she worked tirelessly to provide for her children, to feed them, and to create a semblance of normalcy. But her challenges deepened when she made a horrifying discovery—a dead calf had been thrown into the water well she used to draw water for her family.

Who could have committed such a cruel act? Could someone have done it deliberately? Who would be so heartless as to harm a struggling widow and her innocent children? Was it an act of rage tied to the loss of her husband? Or was it, as some speculated, an unthinkable attempt to ease her "burden" of raising her children? The truth of what happened may never be known.

What is known, however, is this: my mom was stronger than anyone could have imagined. She didn't give up. Gathering her children, she left that place behind and found a small, safe home—a haven where she could nurture and protect her beloved children, her pride and joy. She believed each of her children was a gift from God, an answer to her prayers, and she was determined to care for them, no matter the odds.

This young mother became a living testament to strength and faith. Her unwavering trust in God carried her through, and her constant words of reassurance echoed her belief: "The Lord will never leave me or forsake me." These were not just words she spoke—they were truths she lived by, a testimony of her deep faith and resilience.

Deuteronomy 31:6

"Be strong and courageous. Do not be afraid or terrified because of them, for the Lord your God goes with you; he will never leave you nor forsake you."

Words Can Sting, but Faith and Prayers Bring Healing and Comfort

I still remember the day I got on the school bus wearing white bobby socks and bright white canvas sneakers. Mr. Bill Stokely, our kind-hearted bus driver, smiled warmly and complimented my outfit. But then, a young girl's cruel words cut deep: "She may have new shoes, but she doesn't have a daddy." Those words stung. I sat down, tears streaming down my face, and Mr. Bill comforted me, telling me that everything would be okay. His kindness stayed with me, and I'll always remember how he treated me with such care.

That night, as I lay in the middle of the bed with my mom and sister, I said my prayers. I prayed for safety, for my family, and, most of all, for a daddy—someone who would love us, protect us, and never harm us. I trusted God with my deepest hope, even when it seemed impossible.

One afternoon, not long after, I came home from school and grabbed a soda—an Ale-8, a Kentucky favorite—before running out to the field where a man was plowing. Gathering my courage, I asked if he'd like a drink of my soda. He politely declined, but I liked him, so I offered again. This time, he accepted, though he drank a little too much, and my pout must have given me away. He chuckled and, to make it up to me, offered me a ride on his tractor.

It didn't take long for my mother to notice. She came running, scolding me for bothering the man and reminding me never to ask for rides from strangers. But what she didn't know was that moment was no accident—it was an answer to my prayer. That man was Cecil Seale. He would become my daddy.

Cecil was everything I had prayed for: loving, protective, and gentle. He never harmed us. He became the father I had longed for, a gift from God Himself. That day in the field was the beginning of a new chapter for my family, a testament to God's faithfulness and His ability to hear even the quietest prayers of a little girl.

Matthew 7:7-8

"Ask, and it will be given to you; seek, and you will find; knock, and it will be opened to you. For everyone who asks receives, and the one who seeks finds, and to the one who knocks it will be opened."

Facing Nightmares with Hope and Gratitude

When we encounter nightmares—those moments when we're afraid to close our eyes because the darkness feels overwhelming—we often find ourselves searching for light. It's in these moments that we must shift our thoughts toward better, happier times, drawing strength from memories and focusing on life's blessings, even when the days feel hard.

For me, one of the greatest sources of light in my life has been my dad, Cecil. After the loss of my biological father, Cecil came into my life and gave me countless happy moments to cherish. Growing up around him, I learned an invaluable lesson: there are simple, good things in life worth appreciating.

Cecil was a farmer who worked hard for his livelihood. His income came from selling tobacco, which meant that his salary for the year would only arrive during the winter months. He managed his money wisely, carefully distributing it to cover expenses throughout the year. Despite the challenges of farming life, he always found ways to create joyful moments for us as a family.

One of my fondest memories was our annual school

shopping trip each August. My dad had a strong sense of pride in how we presented ourselves, and he insisted that I dress nicely. He wasn't a fan of T-shirts for girls or women—he preferred dress suits, dresses, or crisp white blouses. That shopping trip was always a special treat. After picking out clothes, we would go out to eat at one of his favorite spots, like a buffet or Long John Silver's. I'll never forget the laughter and warmth we shared during those outings—it was a time to celebrate simple joys as a family.

Beyond these moments, my dad's influence extended to how I carry myself each day. He taught me the value of self-care: getting up, bathing, brushing my teeth, ironing my clothes, and dressing well to show respect for myself and for life. Through his example, I learned that even small habits like these reflect an investment in oneself.

My dad's ability to appreciate life's little pleasures, despite its challenges, has shaped who I am. He taught me resilience, gratitude, and the beauty of finding joy in the ordinary.

John 1:5

"The light shines in the darkness, and the darkness has not overcome it."

Memories and Dedication

I don't hold many memories of my biological father. My family rarely spoke about the day he passed away, likely because I struggled with nightmares as a child. I do remember my dad—who raised me—comforting me during those difficult nights. He would come get me from bed, let me sleep with him and my mom, and sometimes stay up with me until I was calm enough to sleep. When the nightmares made me physically sick from fear of the night, he never hesitated to carry me back to bed with care.

At times, I felt like I disappointed my siblings because I had so few memories of my biological father, and those I did have were painful. I recall one vivid moment when my aunt held me and encouraged me to lean down and kiss him goodbye as he lay in his coffin. Another fleeting memory is of me hugging his leg the day he came through the gate to visit us—the very day he died. That's the sum of what I remember about him.

I have pictures of him in his military uniform, and I've often wondered how his life took such a hard turn. He was a WWII veteran. Was it the trauma of war? The loss of his own father? Or the immense burden of being a farmer with eight children? Whatever the reasons, he was broken in spirit and turned to alcohol for solace. My brothers and sister shared only a few stories about their lives, likely because many were overshadowed by the damage alcohol caused in our home. It's heartbreaking to reflect on.

In response to these memories—or the lack thereof—I've dedicated my life to serving others. I work to support veterans, assist those struggling with addiction, and care for the homeless. In doing so, I try to honor all three of my parents: my mom, through my support of widows and the homeless; my biological father, by serving veterans and those battling addiction; and my dad, who raised me by striving to be positive, generous, and loving to all, beyond the bonds of family or DNA.

God has blessed me with the energy and a deep desire to serve, shaped by my life experiences, as well as His teachings in Scripture that inspire my persistence. Verses like James 1:27 resonate deeply with me: "Religion that God our Father accepts as pure and faultless is this: to look after orphans and widows in their distress and to keep oneself from being polluted by the world." This truth has served as a guide for me as I strive to make my life a reflection of His love and grace.

There are simple ways we can each show love and show the love of Christ for all.

Galatians 6:9

"Let us not become weary in doing good, for at the proper time we will reap a harvest if we do not give up."

Passion in Action

As I look back on my childhood, I find myself reflecting on how the experiences and stories that shaped me continue to guide my values today. My biological father, a man I barely knew, leaves behind a legacy that echoes in the stories others have shared with me. He was a soldier, a farmer, and a man of humor—a combination of strength, humility, and joy. Though our time together was limited, his life has left an indelible mark on my own. From his service in the military to the family stories that trace back to the Revolutionary War, I can't help but wonder if my deep respect for the military was planted by his legacy, or if it's something that simply grew within me over time.

I have always admired those who serve in uniform. Their commitment, sacrifice, and resilience inspire me to do what I can to support them. Military service comes with unique challenges that often go unseen by society. Young men and women are sent across the globe, far from their families, sometimes seeing them only once or twice a year. Military families stationed abroad learn to lean on friends and neighbors, building their own communities because their loved ones are not nearby. Too often, we as a society forget the incredible sacrifices not just of the service members, but of their families who support them from the home front. I strive never to forget, and I work diligently to provide respect, encouragement, and tangible support wherever I can.

It's fascinating to think about how passions like these develop. Is it something passed down through bloodlines, like my father's service and the military history of his family? Or is it a quiet calling that grows with time and experience? As I reflect, I recognize that no matter the origin, my passion for supporting the military is something I hold deeply. And there are so many ways to show our support—through prayer for their safety, through kindness and encouragement, and through charitable contributions to organizations that serve our soldiers and their families. One organization that is especially close to my heart is Army Emergency Relief. I've witnessed firsthand how this program steps in during times of need, offering financial support to military members when they face unexpected challenges. It's a lifeline for those who have given so much of themselves.

At the heart of this reflection lies a simple truth: whatever cause we are passionate about, we should honor it with action. Whether it's the military, healthcare, education, or another worthy cause, our passions are a gift that reminds us to serve others in meaningful ways. It's not just about what we do, but about the spirit with which we do it—serving with love, humility, and gratitude. In the end, I'm grateful for the passion I have for supporting our military. It's a small way to give back to those who have given so much. Whether my passion is born from my father's legacy or something else entirely, I am proud to honor it and strive to live it out each day. This brings to mind the teaching of Christ in Scripture. Christ teaches us to support those in need, especially those who sacrifice so much for others, as our efforts in support are a reflection of God's love in action.

Hebrews 13:16

"Do not forget to do good and to share with others, for with such sacrifices God is pleased."

Cherished Memories

When I married and moved to Germany, I found myself in a foreign land where I didn't speak the language. Thankfully, being surrounded by military personnel offered a sense of community, as many were kind and supportive of young spouses like me. I often reflect on those days in Germany with gratitude for the kindness shown by so many.

One story I frequently share is about a rainy day when I walked to the barracks to pick up mail. We lived in Nuremberg, and my husband's barracks were in Zirndorf, which meant taking the bus and walking to and from the bus stop. On that particular day, the rain poured down, and I was wearing nothing more than a small leather jacket. A soldier stopped and kindly offered me a ride.

As we talked during the drive to my apartment, I mentioned that my husband was in the field and invited the soldier to join us for dinner on Saturday once my husband returned. He accepted the invitation and asked if he could bring a few friends. I assured him there would be plenty of food.

When my husband came home, I told him we were expecting guests and described the soldier who gave me a ride. I added that he wore an eagle on his collar. My husband's eyes widened, and he explained the eagle meant the soldier was a Colonel—specifically, the Brigade Commander!

Saturday arrived, and we prepared a humble meal of hot dogs and chips. To my surprise, the commander and his wife brought brownies, accompanied by the Command Sergeants Major and my husband's First Sergeant. What started as an impromptu dinner invitation turned into the beginning of a wonderful friendship and deep respect for my husband's leadership team.

We laughed for years about the young corporal's wife inviting the Brigade Command Team over for hot dogs, and I teased my husband about whether he could get an eagle to wear, too. This experience taught me that simple acts of kindness, even when done out of naivety, can create cherished memories and lifelong friendships. When I think of this time, it serves as a reminder that extending kindness without overthinking it can lead to blessings and meaningful connections that we can cherish and hold in our hearts for years to come.

Hebrews 13:2

"Do not forget to show hospitality to strangers, for by so doing some people have shown hospitality to angels without knowing it."

The Power of
Role Models

As a young girl, I remember a time when I overheard my dad giving money to his brother, Victor, who handed him food stamps in return. My dad quietly took the stamps and placed them in an old locker where he kept important things, including cash. I was furious with him. I thought, *Why wouldn't he just loan Victor the money outright?* My frustration grew, and I refused to speak to him for days. In my disappointment, I questioned the man I had always looked up to. I expected better.

A few days later, my parents were heading to a nearby town for grocery shopping. On the way, we stopped at Victor's house. I watched from the car as my dad walked up to the door and handed the food stamps to Virginia, Victor's wife. It clicked. My dad hadn't taken the stamps for himself—he had simply found a discreet way to return them to Victor's family.

As he climbed back into the car, I couldn't hold back a smile. I hugged him tightly, and though he didn't ask why, I silently resolved to carry his example in my own life. That's who my dad was—a man of integrity, selflessness, and love.

This is the same man who married a widow with eight children and raised them as his own, pouring his heart into a family that needed him. His quiet acts of kindness taught me more about generosity and compassion than words ever could. As I navigate this world, I strive to emulate his character, becoming someone others can respect, learn from, and love.

We all need role models, and I'm grateful mine is my dad.

Philippians 2:4

"Each of you should look not only to your own interests, but also to the interests of others."

Healing through Memories

As a child, I often wondered how my life would turn out. Could I overcome the trauma of seeing my biological father shot? Could I forget the feeling of kissing his forehead as he lay in his coffin? That memory remains as vivid today as the day it happened. For years, I harbored anger toward my aunt, the one who held me and had me kiss his forehead. I don't know why she did that. I'm sure it wasn't meant to harm me. Perhaps she believed it would help me show my love for him or that I would someday cherish the moment. But instead, I remember the coldness of his forehead. That isn't the kind of memory a child wants to keep of her father.

Childhood memories often fade with time, but the ones rooted in great joy or deep sorrow tend to remain. The challenge—and the opportunity—is not letting the sad moments overshadow the good ones. Reflecting on both the painful and happy memories, I've learned how they shape our lives. They can inspire us to create moments of joy, for ourselves and others.

I often think that part of my healing has come from my desire to serve others. It has driven me to create opportunities for happiness and joy, both big and small. God has blessed me with the ability to love deeply and to strive to bring light to others' lives.

When I reflect on how my life has turned out, I am profoundly grateful. God has strengthened me, guiding and leading me through every trauma I've faced, both as a child and an adult. His grace has transformed my pain into purpose, allowing me to bring hope and love to those around me.

Psalm 147:3

"He heals the brokenhearted and binds up their wounds."

Reflection of a Brother's Kindness

When I think about my childhood, it is impossible not to reflect on the profound impact of my brothers. Throughout my life, my brothers have stood as a beacon of kindness and support. It was obvious they loved me deeply, and their love was evident in the way they cared for me.

As a child, I often received thoughtful gifts that made me feel special—sweaters, watches, and pendants that reflected their generous spirit. Later, as a single mother, I relied on their quiet acts of support. My brothers would show up with necessities like milk, bread, and bacon, always ensuring that my needs were met. Their generosity wasn't about grand gestures but rather their unwavering presence and willingness to help.

My brothers were strong children who grew into even stronger men, both physically and emotionally. Despite their strength, what stood out most was their gentle and kind heart. My brothers lived with a tenderness that was rare and cherished, showing their love through action, care, and unwavering encouragement.

When I reflect on his life, I see the beauty of someone whose greatest strength lay not in their physicality but in the kindness shared. My brothers' example reminds me that among all the gifts and attributes a person might possess, the most beautiful is a spirit of kindness and love for others. Their life stands as a testament to the power of gentleness and compassion, especially in their relationship with their siblings.

My brothers' legacy will always remind me of this truth: it is not our achievements or possessions that define us, but the love and kindness we share.

Galatians 5:22-23

"But the fruit of the Spirit is love, joy, peace, forbearance, kindness, goodness, faithfulness, gentleness, and self-control. Against such things, there is no law."

When the Spirit Whispers Comfort

Some days are harder than others, and on a particular day, I had one of those days. I had been carrying some medical concerns I could not talk about. The weight of it pressed on me as I sat in Church, tears threatening to spill over. It felt like my emotions were sitting right at the edge, just waiting for a moment to break free.

But isn't it something how God works through the people in our lives?

On this day, I came home and found a song sent by a friend. As I listened, it was as if I was sitting with my friends from my younger days—laughing, chatting, reminiscing. I felt their presence so clearly, those friends who have gone before me and those still here loving me.

When my son was in the ICU, I remember crying myself to sleep, but in those moments, I'd feel comfort from the memories of those we love, even those who passed on and are no longer with us. It's amazing how we can comfort ourselves with our memories of those who have passed on when we need it most. And for those still here, they seem to have an uncanny sense of when we need a hug—even if it's just through words or a song.

Often when I am down, I think how Scripture reminds me of the unbreakable bonds of love and loyalty—both with those who are still walking this earth with us and with those who have gone on ahead. These connections don't fade with time or distance; they endure, sustained by the love and spirit God places in each of us.

Hold tight to the truth the Lord gives us: He will never leave us or forsake us. His love is reflected in the ones He's placed in our lives to walk beside us, even if only in spirit. Today, I felt that love, and it reminded me I'm never truly alone.

When you find yourself facing something heavy, may you feel the arms of love and spirit around you, too. As I reflect on this day and the love shown to me, I think of Ruth's words to Naomi:

Ruth 1:16

"Don't urge me to leave you or to turn back from you. Where you go, I will go, and where you stay, I will stay. Your people will be my people and your God my God."

The Healing Journey

There was a time in my life when I felt as though moving forward was impossible. My heart was heavy, burdened by sadness and worry for my son. My son was incredibly close to his dad. When his dad passed away from cancer at a young age, it devastated all three of our children—but it shattered my son's world.

My son struggled deeply with his grief. As the years went on, his pain led him down a dark path, and he became addicted to street drugs. As his mother, I prayed endlessly for him. I searched for him in the streets, desperate to find him and bring him home, hoping to save him from the darkness that consumed him.

In 2002, my world came crashing down. My son was shot in the face. I will never forget the phone call or the doctors telling me how critical his condition was. They said he might not make it. My heart broke in a way I cannot describe. My son was placed in a coma, and as he lay in the ICU, I clung to prayer. I begged God to heal him, to give him another chance. God answered my prayers. Against all odds, my son survived.

Now, 24 years later, we are facing another battle—liver disease resulting from hereditary hemochromatosis. Some moments, I feel strong and hopeful, but there are other moments when I just want to cry. As a mother, all I want is to take the pain, the fear, and the worry from my child. I want my son to be healthy, to be safe, to live without this burden. Waiting for treatment that may lead to healing is excruciating. Yet, even in the uncertainty, I remind myself to trust in the Lord. He is the Great Physician, the ultimate healer, and the comforter of our souls. I continue to pray for my son's healing and for peace in my heart. I lean on my faith, knowing that God is in control. We must remember that our God promises His strength and support during trials.

Jeremiah 30:17

"But I will restore you to health and heal your wounds,' declares the Lord."

Unconditional Love Heals the Brokenhearted

I recall a time in my life when the emotional pain felt endless. It wasn't physical pain, but a hurt that cut deep. It stemmed from words that may not have been meant to harm, yet they did. I was just a young girl, wearing a new pair of boots and a skirt my mom had bought for me. She had taken me to the local grocery store to pick up a snack for school. As I browsed the aisles, I overheard someone say, "Yeah, that's the youngest of the children whose father was killed." The words stung. I silently picked out my candy bar, paid for it, and left the store.

Later, I asked the man I called Dad—the one who raised me—why he hadn't adopted us. Deep down, I believed that if he had adopted us and changed our last names, we would be seen differently. We'd be known as his children, not as the children of the man who was killed. His response was something I have treasured my entire life. He said, "Sissy, your name or a piece of paper doesn't make you my daughter. The way I love you makes you mine."

Those words became an anchor in my heart; a constant reminder of the deep love my dad had for me. Over time, I came to understand how much those words also honored my biological dad. My dad saw no need to change my name or create a legal document to prove his love and commitment to me and my siblings. His actions spoke louder than any paperwork could. He loved us unconditionally. He loved my mom, a widow with eight children, with the kind of boundless kindness and devotion that still amazes me. When I reflect on his love, I'm reminded of the way God loves us—without conditions. God doesn't need legal proof or outward gestures; He simply asks us to seek Him, believe in Him, confess our sins, and live for Him.

I pray that God strengthens me daily to live a life that reflects His love—a life that also mirrors the unconditional love my dad showed me. It was his love that helped ease the pains of life and what continues to inspire me. What a priceless gift my dad was and remains to this day. As I reflect on his love, it shapes who I am and challenges me to love others in the same way.

I pray to live a life that not only pleases Christ, but it is also a life lived that makes my dad (s) proud. I pray that when heartache shows its face, physical or emotional, we remain focused on the great love our Heavenly Father has for each of us, each of his children.

> **1 John 3:1**
>
> **"See what great love the Father has lavished on us, that we should be called children of God! And that is what we are!"**

Blessings of God

Life offers countless opportunities to witness God at work. While we often focus on monumental, life-changing events, He frequently reveals His presence and love in the most unexpected ways and moments.

When I was younger, juggling work and pursuing a degree, I decided to write down a bucket list: a collection of dreams and goals I hoped to achieve in life. Among the aspirations on that list were pursuing a master's degree, eventually a doctorate, owning a Lincoln, and having a fur coat. I also included trips and concerts I dreamed of experiencing. Over time, I kept these goals in mind and worked toward them, accomplishing many along the way.

Years later, as I was searching for my thesis from graduate school, I stumbled across that old bucket list. Reading through it, I was humbled and moved to tears. I couldn't believe how materialistic my list had been. Overwhelmed, I asked God to forgive me for placing so much value on worldly possessions. That evening, I shared the discovery with my husband and told him about my prayer for forgiveness.

Later that night, a friend unexpectedly reached out to me. She shared that her mother had passed away and left behind several fur coats. She asked if I would like to see them. When I tried them on, I was astonished—there weren't just one or two coats, but five. I couldn't believe it. The same night I had asked God to forgive me for my materialism, He had blessed me with something that had once been a dream of my heart.

That moment was a profound reminder: God knows our hearts. He loves us and provides not only for our needs but often blesses us with the desires of our hearts, even when we least expect it. God has been so good to me, always providing and always reminding me of His unfailing love. When we surrender to God and align our hearts with Him, He blesses us in ways that reflect both His love and His abundant grace.

Psalm 37:4

"Delight yourself in the Lord, and He will give you the desires of your heart."

Finding Purpose
in Work

As a child, I often wondered how life would turn out. Would I marry? Have children? Pursue a fulfilling career? So many questions filled my young mind, each carrying its own sense of wonder. Eventually, life led me to a career in military housing, though at the time, I could not have predicted how much it would shape my purpose.

My journey began humbly, but it didn't take long for me to realize I truly enjoyed my work. I discovered a passion for serving others—specifically, Soldiers and their Families. The job allowed me to learn, research, strategize, plan, and implement programs that would make a tangible difference in their lives. What a blessing it was to do work that mattered, day in and day out.

I found joy in improving barracks and housing, in setting standards of operation, and in inspiring teams to achieve shared goals. More than anything, I cherished contributing to the quality of life for the men and women who dedicate their lives to service. It became clear to me that this work wasn't just a job; it was a calling.

Reflecting on my journey, I am reminded of how important it is to find purpose in what we do. Life is short, and each of us has a unique role to play. Sometimes, that purpose is found in our current work, in the people we meet, the problems we solve, and the lives we touch. Other times, it means stepping into something new to discover what truly ignites our passion.

My advice to others is this: don't just work—live. Reflect on each day and ask yourself: Is this where my heart lies? Is this where God is calling me? If not, have the courage to seek the place where your gifts can shine.

I remember the wisdom of my father when I took my very first job, serving ice cream. He told me, "When you're not serving, find something to do—sweep, clean, never let your hands be idle. If you work hard and stay busy, you'll always have a job." That simple lesson stuck with me and shaped my approach to every task since.

As I reflect, I am reminded of Scripture that speaks to diligence and purpose:

"Whatever you do, work heartily, as for the Lord and not for men." (Colossians 3:23)

We are here for a reason. Whether serving ice cream, improving housing, or leading others, our work can have eternal value if we commit it to God and strive to serve others with a genuine heart.

> **Proverbs 16:3**
>
> **"Commit your work to the Lord, and your plans will be established."**

Responding with Kindness

In life and work, we sometimes encounter people who are not kind. They may be ornery, dishonest, selfish, self-serving, or even jealous. I have met such individuals. For me, this was particularly evident during an internship program where I was hired with the understanding that I would be progressively promoted upon completing each phase of training. This structured advancement didn't sit well with some of my peers.

One manager openly voiced their frustration, saying, "You come in with college degrees, get trained through an accelerated program, and move up quickly, while we've been here working hard without the same opportunities." This resentment led to intentional challenges during my internship, and it became clear that the internship program wasn't widely appreciated or supported by the workforce.

So, what should we do when faced with situations like this? How should we respond when we are the target of others' frustrations? This is where reflection is essential. Remember the "WWJD" armbands—What Would Jesus Do? Pausing to reflect on Scripture can guide our response. However, we are human, and sometimes our initial reaction is anger or defensiveness. But what if we chose to respond with empathy, understanding, and kindness instead? My pastor often says, "It is easy to act like a Christian, but more difficult to react like a Christian."

When life presents such challenges, I propose that before reacting, we take a moment to reflect on what Christ would have us do. Scripture offers wisdom and guidance that we can apply to scenarios like this:

"Do not be overcome by evil, but overcome evil with good." (Romans 12:21)

When faced with hostility or resentment, respond with grace and goodness rather than retaliation. Overcome the negativity by exemplifying Christ's love and patience.

"A gentle answer turns away wrath, but a harsh word stirs up anger." (Proverbs 15:1)

Responding calmly and gently can diffuse tension. By maintaining composure, we reflect Christ's peace and invite reconciliation rather than further conflict.

"Bless those who persecute you; bless and do not curse." (Romans 12:14)

Responding with Kindness

Even when others seem against us, we are called to bless them. Pray for those who create challenges, asking God to work in their hearts as well as ours.

"Be completely humble and gentle; be patient, bearing with one another in love." (Ephesians 4:2)

Humility and patience are powerful tools. Instead of dwelling on the unfairness, we must focus on demonstrating love and understanding, even when it's difficult. We must remember who we ultimately serve. Excellence and integrity in our work are acts of worship, regardless of others' opinions or treatment. By applying these principles, we can turn difficult situations into opportunities to reflect Christ's character. Let us strive to meet resentment with understanding, hostility with kindness, and challenges with faith. When we pause, reflect, and pray before responding, we allow God's wisdom to guide us—and that's a response that honors Him.

Colossians 3:23

"Whatever you do, work at it with all your heart, as working for the Lord, not for human masters."

The Call to Lay Down My Net

It was a crisp Wednesday evening as I entered the church. The pastor's sermon focused on Matthew 4:18-22, the story of Jesus calling Simon, called Peter, and Andrew, his brother, to lay down their nets and follow Him. As the pastor shared the Scripture, I listened, but my heart was heavy. I tried to stay focused, but my mind was with my son, my son. Worry had taken root in my soul, and no matter how many times I whispered prayers over the past few days, it lingered like a stubborn shadow.

Then, the pastor's reading of the Scripture was clearly heard and took hold of my mind.

"As Jesus was walking beside the Sea of Galilee, he saw two brothers, Simon called Peter and his brother Andrew. They were casting a net into the lake, for they were fishermen. 'Come, follow me,' Jesus said, 'and I will send you out to fish for people.' At once, they left their nets and followed him. Going on from there, he saw two other brothers, James, the son of Zebedee, and his brother John. They were in a boat with their father Zebedee, preparing their nets. Jesus called them, and immediately they left the boat and their father and followed him."

The pastor paused and asked our thoughts on this Scripture. I responded, "Those nets weren't just tools for catching fish. They symbolized safety, routine, even identity. Leaving them behind meant leaving behind fear, control, and worry. Jesus was asking them to trust Him fully, to let go of what was holding them back, and to step into something new, unknown, but deeply purposeful."

I sat there, absorbing his words, but my mind drifted to my son. As his mother, I longed to be by his side, to hold him, to shield him from harm. But my son had asked for space, and I had promised to honor his wish. My heart ached. I wanted so badly to fix things, to wrap him in the safety of my arms, but I knew I couldn't.

The pastor's voice broke through my thoughts. "What's your net? What are you holding on to that keeps you from fully trusting God? Is it fear? Worry? Addiction? Whatever it is, lay it down at His feet. Trust Him to lead you, to carry what you cannot bear."

I realized in that moment that my net was fear—fear

for my son's health, fear of the unknown, fear that my absence might somehow make him lonely, or in need. But I also remembered God's promises.

"For God has not given us a spirit of fear, but of power and of love and of a sound mind." (2 Timothy 1:7)

I breathed deeply, whispering the words in my heart. God loved my son first, and He loves him most. I had to trust that God was with him, holding him close, even when I couldn't. Tears filled my eyes. I didn't need to carry the weight alone. God cares for my son. He cares for me. I closed my eyes and prayed, surrendering my net to Him.

"Lord, I trust You. I trust You to protect my son, to hold him close, and to heal him in Your time. I will lean on You. But Father, You know my heart. It hurts to be apart from him. Help me honor his wishes and wait until he is ready. Give me peace in the waiting, and remind me that You are always with me, always in control."

If and when trouble and concern present themselves, remember that your worries may not be gone, but we know where to place them. When fear tries to creep in, hold tightly to His promises:

> **Psalm 28:7**
>
> "**The Lord is my strength and my shield; my heart trusts in Him, and He helps me. My heart leaps for joy, and with my song I praise Him.**"

A Son's Journey

There are days that can be a challenge. On one particular day, my son had been on my mind constantly, and my heart was heavy with concern for him. His diagnosis was a terrifying reality. We did not know the stage, the plan of attack, or how he would be feeling from one day to the next. The uncertainty during this illness impacting his liver, could be nerve-wracking.

Driving home after work, I decided to call my son. In hindsight, it wasn't my best decision. He had spent the prior day at the hospital for lab work and was struggling to sleep. I sent him a heating pad, hoping it might help ease his pain. But when I called, I learned he had invited a friend over to play games on the computer—and they were drinking. My son was intoxicated.

I was angry and heartbroken. Part of me wanted to be his mom and tell him not to drink, especially knowing the toll it could take on his body, especially with liver disease. But I knew it wasn't the time for an argument. I see the grip of addiction and how it harms, just as smoking and drinking do. Both are devastating. As a mother, my concerns for my children are deep and unending.

Despite my heartache, I'm reminded of God's love, which gives us hope and strength even in the darkest times. I must trust that God is holding my son in His hands. I prayed for my son to feel God's peace and for the courage to make choices that protect his health.

As I reflected on my day, the Parable of the Prodigal Son came to mind (Luke 15:11-32). It's a parable I have relied on many times during my years with my son. It reminds me of the love a parent has for their child—a love that is unwavering and unconditional, even in the face of heartache. Like the father in the story, I knew I would always welcome my children with open arms and a heart full of love, no matter how difficult the journey becomes.

I hold onto this promise, believing that God has a plan for our lives, and that of our children, one filled with hope and healing. I trust Him to guide us through life's journey, no matter how uncertain or difficult it may feel.

We are to pray for those battling diseases, for healing, strength, and the ability to overcome both liver disease and the struggles that weigh the healing down.

Jeremiah 29:11

"For I know the plans I have for you," declares the Lord, "plans to prosper you and not to harm you, plans to give you hope and a future."

The Weight of the Night

During the journey of knowing my son has hereditary hemochromatosis, the nights can be long— one particular night, I had stomach issues that kept me up all night. But deep within, I know that's just the Devil trying to shake me. Not today, Satan. That's my mantra, not today, Satan. I cried out that I rebuke him in the mighty name of Jesus! I will stand firm, go to Church, and cry out to God with every ounce of faith I have.

I will cry out for healing—for my son, and for my friends. God WILL win. I will trust His plan, His power, and His love. They will all be better; they will have the eyes of the Lord upon them, and they will be blessed in the name of our Heavenly Father. God wins EVERY time.

"The Lord is a warrior; the Lord is His name."
—Exodus 15:3

In this battle, I stand as part of His army, equipped with the armor of God:

"Be strong in the Lord and in His mighty power. Put on the full armor of God, so that you can take your stand against the Devil's schemes."—Ephesians 6:10-11

As my son faces his battle with liver disease, I hold to this:

"The Lord will fight for you; you need only to be still."—Exodus 14:14

God is our healer, our refuge, and our strength. I rebuke the enemy and declare victory through Christ. We are warriors of faith, and we will not be defeated. God's hand is on my son, my friends, and my family. Healing is coming! AMEN.

I will cling to my faith! I will show unshakeable trust in God's promises and His ultimate victory. Even in the midst of trials, I will stand firm, proclaiming healing, and clinging to His Word. I will face the night with the spirit and faith of a warrior in God's Army!

Faith will move mountains, and our prayers are mighty. I will hold onto His truth, knowing that He is with me, my son, and my friends every step of the way. He is Jehovah Rapha, our Healer, and He hears the cries of our heart for my son, my friends, Brenda, Chad, and Rose. God WILL show up, and He WILL move in miraculous ways.

I will take heart in His promises, such as Isaiah

41:10: "So do not fear, for I am with you; do not be dismayed, for I am your God. I will strengthen you and help you; I will uphold you with my righteous right hand."

We are covered in His armor and fortified by His power. Cry out to Him, and rest in His embrace, knowing that the victory is already won. I will pray for healing, peace, and strength each day of my life, and I will trust in the healing power of my God.

Psalm 147:3

"He heals the brokenhearted and binds up their wounds."

A Mother's Prayer: Holding Onto Faith in the Face of Uncertainty

As a mother, there is no deeper ache than watching your child battle an illness that you cannot fix. The helplessness, the constant stream of prayers whispered in the quiet moments, and the deep yearning for healing—these are emotions only a mother who has walked this road can truly understand.

I find myself in this place: praying fervently for my son's healing from liver disease while wrestling with the reality that healing may not come on this side of Heaven. It's a thought that tears at my heart, yet it also invites me to lean deeper into my faith, to look beyond the physical and cling to the eternal promises of God.

But how do I accept this? How do I hold on to my faith if the healing I long for doesn't happen in this lifetime?

The answer, I think, begins with understanding the nature of God's healing. Healing doesn't always look the way we imagine. Sometimes, it's physical and miraculous, a restoration we can see and touch. Other times, it's a release from pain, a restoration of peace, and a complete renewal in the presence of God. It's hard to grasp, but I have to believe that no matter how God chooses to heal, His way is good, even when it's not the way I would choose.

Will I be able to see God's healing if it doesn't happen here? Yes. Because I trust that in Heaven, there is no sickness, no pain, and no suffering. My son will be whole, radiant, and free. And though that thought brings tears to my eyes, it also brings a quiet hope to my heart.

Will I see God's presence? Yes, I already do. I see it in the moments of grace that sustain me when I feel too weak to go on. I see it in the prayers of friends and family who stand in the gap when I can barely find the words. I see it in the way God carries my son, even in the hardest moments. His presence is here, even in the pain, even in the questions.

How can I stand strong? Only by leaning into the One who is my strength. By daily surrendering my fears, my doubts, and my broken heart to Him. By remembering that my faith isn't rooted in getting the answers I want, but in trusting the God who loves my son even more than I do.

To honor my faith, I will keep praying. I will keep trusting. I will love my son fiercely and treasure every moment we have together. And if the healing doesn't come here, I will honor God by holding on to the hope that we will see it in eternity.

This journey isn't easy. There are days when the weight feels too heavy, the fear too overwhelming. So, I stand not because I am strong, but because He is. And in the end, whether healing comes here or in Heaven, I know that God is faithful, and He will see us through.

For every mother walking this road, you are not alone. Keep praying, keep hoping, and keep trusting. God's love and presence are with us, even here, even now.

2 Corinthians 12:9

"My grace is sufficient for you, for my power is made perfect in weakness."

Held by His Grace

Some days, it's hard to fathom just how much can come at a person. A nonprofit reached out, asking me to find an investor and sell their properties to cover past-due taxes. The investor agreed, the transaction went through the title company as required, and at closing, two loans were paid off, and a covenant was signed. Everything seemed in order. But after closing—completely unbeknownst to both the buyer and seller—the city presented liens. It's unbelievable.

The stress can be overwhelming, especially when life's burdens pile up all at once. Worry for my granddaughter's health, concern for my son's health as he faces the recent diagnoses of liver disease, my daughter not doing well with her health issues, and then on the same day, the gut-wrenching call—my grandson in the hospital, facing a blockage that may require surgery. When life feels unbearably heavy, we must acknowledge that this world is tough.

But through it all, we must remember that God holds us in His care. He loves us, and we are His children. He will never abandon us. Even in our darkest moments, He is working. We are called to pray, trust, and cling to His promises. His truth remains unchanged, and He will see us through.

No matter what comes, He is faithful. Keep praying, keep trusting, and hold on to His promises.

1 Peter 5:7

"Cast all your anxiety on Him because He cares for you."

Trusting God in the Call to Serve

When the temperature drops below freezing, the Salvation Army opens its doors as a warming station, offering meals and a place to sleep. My friends and I volunteer to serve evening meals, ensuring those in need receive warmth, food, and companionship.

One evening while serving, I meet a middle-aged woman searching for a place to live. It quickly becomes clear that she cannot live alone—she needs assisted living or a nursing home. Unfortunately, the Salvation Army shelter only operates when temperatures fall below freezing, and the next morning, she arrives at my office, still in search of housing. She is uncertain about her finances and how to care for or furnish a home.

I take her back to our shelter, one we manage, but it becomes evident that she also needs medical attention. We get her to the hospital, where they keep her for a few days before discharging her. Soon, she is back on the streets. We find her again and take her back to the hospital. This time, I reach out to the Health Department, requesting a caseworker to help navigate the system and secure a place for her in a nursing home. It seems we have done all we can to help.

Yet, I find myself wondering: Were my efforts truly what God would have me do? Was there more I could have done? How do we discern if God placed someone in our path and if the help we provided was His will?

In times of uncertainty, we must hold on to the lessons of Christ regarding the care of the less fortunate:

Matthew 25:35-36—"For I was hungry and you gave me something to eat, I was thirsty and you gave me something to drink, I was a stranger and you invited me in, I needed clothes and you clothed me, I was sick and you looked after me, I was in prison and you came to visit me."

Hebrews 13:2—"Do not forget to show hospitality to strangers, for by so doing some people have shown hospitality to angels without knowing it."

Proverbs 19:17—"Whoever is kind to the poor lends to the Lord, and He will reward them for what they have done."

Perhaps the answer lies not in questioning if we did enough, but in trusting that when we act in love and service, we are walking in obedience to His call.

> **James 2:15-16**
>
> **"Suppose a brother or a sister is without clothes and daily food. If one of you says to them, 'Go in peace; keep warm and well fed,' but does nothing about their physical needs, what good is it?"**

Faithful Debate

Isn't it interesting how friends can journey through the year, laughing, sharing, and embracing the wonders of life together—only for election season to arrive and tensions to rise? People who are otherwise law-abiding, charitable, and dedicated to their communities can suddenly find themselves in heated debates over politics. Differences in opinions—whether on social issues, defense, or policy—can lead to harsh words and strained relationships.

But I don't believe God wants us to treat each other with hostility, even when we disagree. This includes discussions on topics that go against Scripture. While we are called to stand firm in our faith and uphold His teachings, we are not called to be judges, juries, or argumentative for the sake of proving a point. Instead, we should engage with others in a way that reflects His love and truth.

Here are some Scriptures that guide us in standing for righteousness while remaining respectful and Christlike:

2 Timothy 2:24-25—"And the Lord's servant must not be quarrelsome but must be kind to

everyone, able to teach, not resentful. Opponents must be gently instructed, in the hope that God will grant them repentance, leading them to a knowledge of the truth."

Colossians 4:6—"Let your conversation be always full of grace, seasoned with salt, so that you may know how to answer everyone."

Ephesians 4:29—"Do not let any unwholesome talk come out of your mouths, but only what is helpful for building others up according to their needs, that it may benefit those who listen."

Let's stand firm in truth while extending grace, remembering that our words and actions should always point back to Him.

Matthew 5:16

"Let your light shine before others, that they may see your good deeds and glorify your Father in heaven."

The Heart of a Caregiver

Some days, as a caregiver, the weight of responsibility feels overwhelming. It can be lonely, frustrating, and exhausting. I strive to keep my thoughts selfless, but after 15 years of caring for my brother with special needs, there are moments when his habits, combined with life's pressures, test my patience. Now, as my son faces serious health issues, the stress feels even heavier.

Beyond my brother, I also care for my nephew, who was homeless, battling addiction, and taken advantage of by someone who exploited his disability payments. Then there is my other nephew, a young man who has never truly known stability, love, or the warmth of family. He, too, needs a place to belong.

Through my own experiences—seeing the devastating effects of drugs and alcohol—I chose a different path, dedicating myself to education and avoiding anything that could lead to destruction. I work diligently to provide a home filled with love, care, and support. But the truth is, constantly giving—financially, emotionally, and spiritually—can be draining.

I often wonder why God made me this way. Why can't I say no to those in need? Am I truly helping others out of pure compassion, or is it something deeper?

Do I seek to heal my own heart, to feel closer to Christ, to find forgiveness? I know that salvation is not earned through works, so why do I push myself to do good?

Perhaps the answer lies not in questioning the why, but in trusting the Who. God has placed this calling on my life, and even when the burden feels heavy, He promises that my labor is not in vain. The love I give, the sacrifices I make, and the care I provide—though exhausting at times—are reflections of His love working through me.

So, I hold onto faith. I keep going, not for recognition or reward, but because love—true, Christ-centered love—is never wasted.

2 Thessalonians 3:13

"But as for you, brothers and sisters, do not grow weary in doing good."

A Call to Serve: Restoring Hope in the Face of Uncertainty

I received a call from a friend with troubling news—the local homeless shelter had closed, and even if it reopened, it was set to shut down again soon. On top of this, I learned that the Salvation Army Shelter would also be closing for a year-long renovation, leaving no emergency shelter available for those in need.

Having witnessed firsthand how many lives had been impacted by the shelter in recent months, I felt an undeniable pull to take action. I approached the shelter's board—already in the process of dissolving—and asked if they had a plan for its future. Their answer was simple: they did not. Not only was the shelter closing, but the entire organization was being dissolved along with all its assets.

I urged them to find a way to sustain operations, but if that wasn't possible, I was willing to try and self-fund to keep the shelter open—because the community needs it. The situation was complicated; though the organization I created was a nonprofit, it was not tax-exempt, meaning a direct transfer wasn't possible. However, they could lease the building that housed the shelter.

Beyond that, I discovered deeper issues—the organization that was dissolving had property it needed to sell to pay off delinquent taxes for 2022, 2023, and 2024. The financial mismanagement and lack of oversight from leadership had left the shelter in crisis.

How does this happen? How does an organization designed to help others fall into such disarray? The answer lies in accountability, transparency, and effective leadership. Without these, even the most well-intentioned missions can falter.

As we work to serve those in need, we must stay vigilant in our stewardship. Providing shelter and hope is not just about funding—it's about responsibility, integrity, and unwavering commitment to the mission. Because when we care for the least among us, we reflect the heart of Christ.

Proverbs 19:17

"Whoever is generous to the poor lends to the Lord, and He will repay him for his deed."

Praying, Planning, and Protecting

During my years working with the Army, I was blessed with an incredible career, doing work that I truly enjoyed. In my early years, I focused on planning renovation projects for barracks, family housing, and lodging. Later, my work expanded to include golf courses, playgrounds, fitness centers, bowling alleys, recreation areas, and parks. I found great fulfillment in developing programs and services that enhanced the lives of our Soldiers and their Families.

After retiring, I quickly realized the challenges that come with planning for an entire community. There seemed to be no unified vision that truly engaged and gained the support of residents. Instead, negativity was widespread. Issues like drug addiction, poverty, broken families, and a struggling education system were evident. Our state ranked 50th in the nation for education and 46th in overall health and well-being—deeply concerning statistics that reflected the urgent needs in our community, state, and nation.

Now, we are facing legislative proposals that would further harm the most vulnerable among us. Bills are being introduced to limit support for homelessness in communities with fewer than 300,000 people—effectively turning a blind eye to those in desperate need. Additionally, a senator has authored a bill that would eliminate speech therapy, occupational therapy, and even vaccinations for children in our schools. These measures do not serve the well-being of our communities but instead place even greater burdens on those already struggling.

Scripture reminds us of our responsibility to pray for our leaders. When the world around us feels broken due to leadership or societal struggles, we must turn to prayer. Pray for intervention, for wisdom among leaders, and for hearts to change. But beyond prayer, we must also act—holding fast to the things we can do to create positive change in the communities we love.

1 Timothy 2:1-2

"I urge, then, first of all, that petitions, prayers, intercession and thanksgiving be made for all people—for kings and all those in authority, that we may live peaceful and quiet lives in all godliness and holiness."

Faith in the Midst of Sudden Loss

Life can change in an instant, reminding us how fragile and unpredictable our time on earth truly is.

My grandson came to my house to work on an essay for his college scholarship, writing about his goals and plans for furthering his education. In the middle of his writing, he received a text from a friend—their parent had passed away.

My grandson was heartbroken. He wanted to rush to his friend's side, to offer comfort, to do something—but I knew the scene would be overwhelming, with law enforcement and the medical examiner present. I gently told him it wasn't the right time. He was sad, feeling helpless, wanting to know how to support his friend through this unimaginable loss. And in that moment, I had no perfect words, no easy answers.

Grief, especially when sudden and devastating, is hard to navigate. Losing a parent so unexpectedly brings a unique kind of pain, one that shakes the foundation of a person's heart. But in these moments of sorrow, we must hold on to faith, trusting in Christ's promises.

Faith Woven With Hope and Conviction

When faced with loss, we must lean into God's presence. Here are a few ways to help as we navigate grief:

- Lean on Prayer—In sorrow, words may fail, but God understands the cries of the heart. Encourage those grieving to pray, even when they don't know what to say.

- Surround Yourself with Support—No one should walk through grief alone. Be present, offer a listening ear, and remind them that love and support are all around.

- Hold on to God's Promises—Scripture reminds us that this world is not the end. There is hope beyond the pain, and God has prepared something greater than we can imagine.

- Give Yourself Grace—Grief has no timeline. It comes in waves, and it's okay to feel lost. God's grace is sufficient even in the moments when faith feels distant.

- Acts of Comfort—Sometimes, the best way to support someone in grief is through simple, loving actions—bringing a meal,

writing a note, or just sitting with them in silence.

Tragedy reminds us how quickly life can change, but it also calls us to trust in the eternal love of Christ. Even in the darkest valleys, we are never alone.

1 Corinthians 2:9

"But as it is written, Eye hath not seen, nor ear heard, neither have entered into the heart of man, the things which God hath prepared for them that love him."

Compassionate Friends, Proud Moments

I could not have been more proud than when my grandson wrote an essay about his encounter with a young person living in the shelter we manage. In his writing, he shared how, before that meeting, he had never given much thought to homelessness; what it truly meant to be without a parent, without a home, and without a sense of security. But meeting someone his own age with no family and no home changed everything.

Through their conversation, my grandson gained a deeper understanding of the struggles many face. His perspective shifted, and with it, his heart. He now carries a newfound compassion for those experiencing homelessness, recognizing that behind every hardship is a person with a story, a soul deserving of kindness.

This chance meeting between the young man and my grandson became a moment of lasting impact— one that will shape his worldview for years to come. It serves as a powerful reminder of the importance of empathy and the call to love one another.

Deuteronomy 15:7-8

"If among you, one of your brothers should become poor, in any of your towns within your land that the Lord your God is giving you, you shall not harden your heart or shut your hand against your poor brother, but you shall open your hand to him and lend him sufficient for his need, whatever it may be."

Beyond Housing:
More than Shelter

I had a discussion that was thought-provoking—it centered on how addressing homelessness can be strengthened through relationships. Without a doubt, relationships matter. I have personally witnessed their impact in helping individuals transition from the streets into stable housing. I have learned through the support of many who were homeless that trust, support, and genuine connection can make all the difference.

Yet, homelessness is complex. I am both a student and a firm believer in the Housing First model. Providing housing is the critical first step, but as Dr. Jack Tsai reminds us, "Housing First is not housing only." Stability requires more than just shelter—it necessitates a holistic approach, including access to healthcare for both physical and mental well-being, employment opportunities, and spiritual or faith-based support.

But how does a community ensure real transformation? It includes establishing relationships, not just with those in need of support, but those actively providing support. It also must include promoting responsibility and ensuring continued support:

Faith Woven With Hope and Conviction

Personal connections are powerful and help build necessary relationships. Community members can engage with those experiencing homelessness through mentorship programs, job training partnerships, or simply showing up consistently to serve meals, listen, and encourage. The smallest act of kindness can restore dignity and trust. There are many opportunities to serve meals and support those in need, such as volunteering at local shelters or providing outreach to those in need.

Equipping individuals with tools for independence is key. This can include vocational training, financial literacy classes, and accountability partnerships that help them rebuild their lives. Proverbs 14:23 reminds us, "All hard work brings a profit, but mere talk leads only to poverty." Work and purpose are essential components of lasting change.

Transitioning from homelessness to stability is not a one-time event; it's a process. Long-term support can come through partnerships with local businesses for employment, faith communities for guidance, and mental health services to address deeper challenges.

Housing is the beginning, but relationships, responsibility, and continued support are what truly transform lives. When a community stands together—investing in people, fostering accountability, and staying committed—the cycle of homelessness can be broken, and hope can be restored. Reflecting on today is a reminder that God's guidebook, the Bible, is a great manual with lessons on how we should live our lives, both when we struggle and when we encounter those we can serve.

Proverbs 3:27

"Do not withhold good from those to whom it is due, when it is in your power to act."

Kindness During
A Veteran's Journey

There are moments when frustration sets in as we navigate the complex processes and procedures of agencies meant to assist those in need. Recently, a young veteran found himself in such a situation. He had left his home state to return to Oklahoma, hoping to be closer to his children. Every penny he had was spent on travel, applications, temporary lodging, and food, leaving him with limited resources and nowhere to turn.

Seeking assistance, he was referred to me. He went to the locations referred to, but they were closed. According to the veteran, despite multiple calls to various agencies, the answer remained the same—there was no help available.

This young man was not just any veteran; he had deployed for more than 36 months, was 100% disabled, and battled the daily challenges of PTSD and other ailments. Just when it seemed hope was slipping away, an investor walked in. Without hesitation, he offered the veteran a home, deferring rent and the deposit until the first of the month. Then, in an act of quiet generosity, he handed him $250 for food.

Overcome with emotion, the veteran wept. The investor simply smiled and said, "This is just money. It's a simple gift. The service you provided our nation is worth far more than anything I have done."

In that moment, I was reminded of a profound truth—while we often look to government services to solve society's problems, the real answer lies in the kindness of our fellow citizens. Compassion, generosity, and a willingness to act can change a life in ways that bureaucracy never will.

Proverbs 3:27

"Do not withhold good from those to whom it is due, when it is in your power to act."

There's Always More Than Meets the Eye

Working with our homeless community is never simple. It's layered with heartbreak, resilience, frustration, and moments of grace. Many people are trying to help—hospitals, shelters, outreach teams, churches, and volunteers—but sometimes, the situation is more complex than just offering a bed or a meal.

While out supporting Girls Night Out Bingo, a fundraiser for our schools, I received a call from a local Pastor who met a lady needing some help. The Pastor explained that the woman who was homeless was in great pain and had nowhere to rest. She had been taken to the hospital but was discharged. The Pastor didn't know what to do. I tried to help, thinking of every option. Finally, I said, "Take her to the shelter—we will support her."

The following morning, my husband and I went to check on her. She was in excruciating pain, suffering from serious medical issues. We took her back to the hospital and got her checked in for an examination, and prayerfully some pain relief and treatment. But she refused blood work. She was angry, hurting, and resistant to care. The doctors were in a tough spot. She wanted pain medication but refused treatment. I stood there and watched it all unfold, feeling the weight of it. I kept thinking—there must be better care for those in critical medical condition, like this woman.

This is the reality we face when we work with the homeless population—people in crisis, scared, hurting, and sometimes unwilling or unable to accept the help they need. It's not as simple as just getting someone into a shelter, a meal, or even a hospital. The human spirit is complicated. I don't share this to place blame. The doctors were doing what they could. The shelter was doing what it could. So many people are working every day to offer support. But the truth is, sometimes, all we can do is stand beside someone in their struggle, offer them dignity, and keep trying. As I reflected on the day and this situation, I recognized I needed prayer, one for sustained compassion, and one for strength. Compassion isn't always easy. But it is always necessary, just as strength and patience are required ingredients for serving others, especially those at the end of life.

A Prayer for Compassion

Heavenly Father, grant us compassionate hearts to serve those in need. Help us see beyond anger, beyond resistance, to the pain and fear within. Let us be Your hands and feet, offering comfort and love to those who have been forgotten or cast aside.

A Prayer for Strength and Patience

Lord, in moments of frustration and exhaustion, give me patience and endurance. Help me to be steady in my mission, to offer kindness even when it is rejected, to remain strong even when the burden feels too heavy. Let me trust in Your plan and lean on Your strength.

Proverbs 3:27

"Do not withhold good from those to whom it is due, when it is in your power to act."

Finding Peace in the Midst of Sacrifice

Some days, I find myself feeling overwhelmed. The workload is heavy, the to-do list never ends, and my house—once my sanctuary—no longer feels like home. The private oasis I once kept in order is now shared with several grown men. I don't share this to complain or to say I don't want them here. I love them, and I know they need me. But I do miss my privacy—the ability to decorate a space, leave it pristine, and return to find it just as I left it.

Sometimes, I simply miss being alone in my own home, enjoying the peace of a clean and welcoming space, ready to host friends and share in joyful fellowship. Is it selfish to feel this way? No, I don't believe it is. It is natural to crave privacy, to long for a beautiful, well-maintained home, and to desire a space where joy, peace, and respite can be found. It is okay to want a place that restores you, a place that feels like home in the truest sense—a refuge not only for others but for yourself as well.

And yet, even in this season of sacrifice and service, I know God sees me. He cares about my heart, my peace, and my joy. Psalm 55:22 reminds me: "Cast your burden on the Lord, and He will sustain you; He will never allow the righteous to be shaken."

So, when I feel less than joyful, I ask for renewed joy, for moments of rest, and for small ways to reclaim peace in my home. I remind myself that I do not have to feel guilty for having desires—for wanting a home that is a source of comfort and not just obligation. I can carve out a quiet corner just for me, fill it with things that bring comfort and beauty. I can step outside more often, take walks, enjoy nature, and breathe deeply. I can play music that soothes my soul, light a candle, or set aside time to visit with friends outside my home.

Even now, in the midst of serving others, I trust that God still desires happiness for me too. God desires for each of us, you and me, to be happy, and he tells us to come to him with the desires of our heart.

John 16:24

Jesus says: "Ask, and you will receive, that your joy may be full."

Comfort for the Hurting and Homeless

Recently, a young woman, only 44 years old, was brought to me seeking shelter. She had been to the hospital in pain, suffering from stage 4 cancer. She was homeless, scared, and battling emotional and mental challenges. In her despair, she was refusing care, but I couldn't let her suffer alone. I insisted she return to the hospital, and by God's grace, she was admitted.

It broke my heart to see someone in such dire need—no home, no family to care for her, and no refuge in a world of abundance. How is it that in a country so blessed, so plentiful, we still have those who are left to suffer, who are forgotten in their time of greatest need?

I asked her if she was a believer. She said yes. So, we prayed. And I continue to pray—Lord, wrap her in Your mercy, hold her close, and bring her comfort in these final days. I also received a message of another great sorrow—a homeless woman, sleeping in a tent near the Salvation Army, passed away. My heart aches.

God, why? Why do we have such sadness, such trauma, such brokenness in our communities? Lord, help us. Open our eyes, stir our hearts, and move our hands to action. Let us not turn away from those in need but instead be Your light in their darkness.

Heavenly Father,

You see the suffering of Your children—the sick, the homeless, the forgotten. You know their pain, their fears, and their silent cries for help. Lord, I lift up this woman and all who find themselves in such desperate situations. Be their refuge, their healer, their peace in the midst of suffering. Let them know they are not alone, that even in their darkest moments, You are near.

God, touch the hearts of those who can help. Give strength to those who serve, those who care, and those who fight for the forgotten. Let our communities not be blind to this pain but rise to meet it with compassion, love, and action.

And for those who have passed, welcome them into Your eternal embrace, where suffering is no more, and love is endless. Teach us, Lord, that we never turn away from those in need, but instead, be vessels of Your love and mercy.

In Jesus' name, Amen.

Proverbs 31:8-9

"Speak up for those who cannot speak for themselves, for the rights of all who are destitute. Speak up and judge fairly; defend the rights of the poor and needy."

Matthew 25:35-36

"For I was hungry and you gave me something to eat, I was thirsty and you gave me something to drink, I was a stranger and you invited me in, I needed clothes and you clothed me, I was sick and you looked after me, I was in prison and you came to visit me."

Finding Hope for
the Forgotten

This particular day was tough. One of our homeless ladies, battling terminal cancer, whom I took to the hospital for care, was being discharged from the hospital with nowhere to go. No nursing home would take her—her past struggles with addiction and a criminal record made her an outcast in a system that often lacks compassion for the most vulnerable.

We learned that the police took her to the hospital a few months earlier, sick and alone, with stage 4 cancer, and brought her to the hospital. But once discharged, she had no place to turn then, and now we are facing it once again. It broke my heart.

With nowhere else to go, I called my Pastor, asked him to pray. He did, and he stayed with me so we could get her into a hotel for the week while we tried to find a solution. But this is a band-aid, not a fix. The reality is devastating—when those with criminal records and addiction histories reach the end of their lives, there is almost no safety net for them.

This is why we must educate our youth about the lasting impact of their choices. The consequences of addiction and crime extend far beyond their worst moments—they follow people when they are sick, old, and alone.

But what can we do for those who are already in this situation? It is unacceptable to leave them dying in the streets. We need real solutions: perhaps we need medical respite care for the homeless, Faith-based rehabilitation programs with housing, a second-chance nursing home system, and Legislation and funding that allows care facilities to accept and rehabilitate people with past criminal records.

This situation is a call to action. The system is broken, but the people of faith, compassion, and action can step in where it fails. How do we build a society that doesn't discard the sick, the homeless, and the forgotten? How can we bring real, lasting solutions? Let's start the conversation. Let's make change happen. Let's remember Scripture that guides us to appropriate action.

Matthew 25:35-36

"For I was hungry and you gave me something to eat, I was thirsty and you gave me something to drink, I was a stranger and you invited me in, I needed clothes and you clothed me, I was sick and you looked after me."

Answered Prayers in Unexpected Ways

Some days are more challenging than others. As I continued working to help our homeless lady battling stage 4 cancer, I faced yet another challenging day. As we continue to care for her, we are busy taking her food and checking in on her, but the reality remains—she desperately needs quality healthcare and hospice care. Navigating this has been difficult, not only because of her medical condition but also due to her criminal history.

Recognizing that I am not a nurse, I knew I needed help. So, I did what I always do—I prayed. I asked God to send the right person at the right time.

Not long after, I received an invitation to lunch from a friend I recently met. My friend who moved here with her husband after he received military orders, joined me. As we talked, I shared my need for a nurse. To my amazement, my new friend revealed that she is a registered nurse and immediately offered to help care for this woman.

At that moment, I was reminded once again of the power of prayer. God provides exactly what we need, exactly when we need it. Today, I witnessed His goodness in action. God is so very good.

> **Philippians 4:19**
>
> **"And my God will supply every need of yours according to his riches in glory in Christ Jesus."**

A Servant's Dilemma: Following God's Call or My Own?

Today was another busy day, and one that reminded me of the complexity of helping others. I needed to visit the woman we've been assisting—a woman battling stage 4 cancer, once homeless, found in a dumpster, and now staying in a hotel with us covering her stay and meals. Despite her fragile condition, she chose to go outside and even invited two people—her brother and his girlfriend—to stay in her room for the night.

A part of me wrestles with this. Should I be upset? Should I expect more gratitude? After all, she was in dire straits, and we worked to get her hospitalized, stabilized, and sheltered. Yet, perhaps in her mind, facing the reality of her illness, she believes these choices no longer matter.

The bigger question lingers in my heart: How do we help those who are terminal, homeless, and struggling, while also guiding them toward grace? Is this truly my burden to bear, or am I overstepping? I often feel that God places people in my path for a reason—that I am meant to help. But am I following His calling, or am I simply following my own desire to fix what is broken?

As we each struggle with when to help and when to step back, when we wonder if it is God's will or our own, what we should always do is pray. Pray for God's guidance. Pray for wisdom and discernment. Lord, help me know when to act and when to trust that You are in control. Let my hands do Your work, but also let my heart rest in Your will.

> **1 Corinthians 15:58**
> "Therefore, my beloved brothers, be steadfast, immovable, always abounding in the work of the Lord, knowing that in the Lord your labor is not in vain."

The Greatest Lesson: Love, Faith, and Listening

It was the first game of our grandson's senior year. Although my husband was not feeling his best, he wanted so badly to go to the game with me, but he struggled. He felt dizzy, out of balance, and at one point, he even said he wasn't sure he'd make it through the night. It broke my heart to hear him say that. He could barely walk.

The following morning, he was a little better, but still not himself. We went to church, and I could see how much he struggled walking in and out. We stopped by a friend's church for their dedication and culture day, and on the way home, he shared that he still felt weak and just . . . off. We talked about how he just needs to rest and take it easy.

When we are struggling with our own health or supporting those we love through their health challenges—like my husband—we often help them most simply by listening. There isn't much I can do to fix how he feels. But I can be kind, supportive, loving, and present. Sometimes, all they need is a safe space to speak their heart.

And that's exactly what happened today. As my husband reflected, our conversation turned to our children and grandchildren—the joy they bring to our lives. Without hesitation, he said, "I am so proud of the father our son is with his boys—teaching them to fish, hunt, and play baseball." Then, with a full heart, he added, "All I ever wanted to teach the kids was how to love Jesus and be a good, honest person."

That brought tears to my eyes because truly, that is the greatest lesson we can pass down.

As I reflected on this discussion, all I could think to do was say thank you to my husband, for being the Dad and Granddad they needed—every single day, in every season of life. We must continue to share stories and experiences that serve as reminders of the importance of teaching our children to love Christ, while we also teach them life skills, which perhaps include fishing, hunting, and embracing their recreational interests, such as baseball.

Galatians 6:2

"Carry each other's burdens, and in this way, you will fulfill the law of Christ."

A Beautiful Union: Love's New Beginning

We attended a beautiful wedding today, dear friends. As we left, we talked about how touching it was to see two people come together in love after a divorce or the loss of a loved one. The bride and groom walked down the aisles separately, from the left and right, and then joined together—symbolizing the different journeys they had traveled before God brought them to each other. It was a truly moving moment.

The bride looked absolutely lovely, but the groom—oh, he was overwhelmed with happiness and love for his bride. It was a reminder of how wonderful it is to find love again, even later in life. As we drove, we reflected on the vows: "'til death do us part." Perhaps God knew we would experience loss, that we would feel lonely, and that we would need companionship again.

Is it okay to move forward and find love after loss? I believe God wants us to be happy, and if that happiness is found in a new marriage, it is not only okay—it is pleasing in God's eyes.

Psalm 147:3

"He heals the brokenhearted and binds up their wounds."

Ecclesiastes 3:1

"To everything there is a season, and a time to every purpose under heaven."

The Heart of Giving

I have a man who was once homeless. He's been housed for about a year and a half now, always pays his rent on time, and often complains about his neighbors. Some days, he's been a challenge. But he also has a habit of bringing me small, thoughtful gifts—his way of showing appreciation.

One night, he called to tell me he had picked up bottles of water, soda, and bags of chips for the monthly tenant meeting I host. I assured him he didn't need to do that, that I already had snacks covered. But he responded, "Brenda, please don't take this away from me. It's something I want to do to help."

My heart ached. These small gestures are his way of giving back, of feeling connected. Coming into the office isn't just about checking in—it's his way of being part of something. This is the same man who sometimes imagines others are talking about him, who gets frustrated over little things, who struggles with his own thoughts. But despite all that, he tries to help me. He quotes Scripture. And in his own way, he reminds me that even in the midst of struggle, the desire to give and belong never fades.

As I reflected on his call, his desire to help, I pondered the simple ways we can help those who are ornery or lonely feel cared for:

Listen with Patience—Sometimes, they just need someone to hear them out, even if they are venting or repeating themselves. Acknowledge Their Efforts—Recognize the good they do, even if it's small. A simple "I appreciate you" can mean a lot.

Include Them in Activities—Invite them to community meetings, church events, or casual gatherings to help them feel connected. Encourage Purpose—Let them contribute in ways that make them feel valued, whether it's setting up chairs, bringing snacks, or sharing their wisdom.

Check In Regularly—A short visit, call, or message can make a difference in their day. Show Kindness in Small Ways—A handwritten note, a cup of coffee, or a thoughtful gesture can brighten their spirits.

Pray with Them (or for Them)—Offering to pray with them or letting them know you are praying for them can provide comfort.

Set Healthy Boundaries with Grace—It's okay to redirect negativity while still showing care and support. Even those who challenge us have hearts that long for connection. Sometimes, their way of showing love is different, but with patience and kindness, we can help them feel seen, valued, and included.

Ephesians 4:32

"Be kind and compassionate to one another, forgiving each other, just as in Christ God forgave you."

Trusting God through Opposition

Wow! The past few days have been quite something. I received a complaint regarding the homeless shelter, and while I will address it, I want to share some perspective. We applied for our tax-exempt status, but the IRS has yet to process it. We've been completely open and honest about this, yet someone still felt the need to complain.

Although our attorneys assured us we could accept donations while awaiting approval, some believe we are taking resources from them and have chosen to throw darts. It is frustrating, but unfortunately, this kind of resistance is common when doing good work. People can be mean, selfish, and self-centered, and it's disheartening when those attitudes get in the way of helping the less fortunate.

So how do you handle negativity when your only goal is to serve others? I remind myself to pause, reflect, and seek understanding before responding. But let's be honest—human emotions make that difficult. The natural reaction is to push back, yet I am learning daily to lean on God. To trust Him.

If He called me to this mission, He will make a way. And I believe He will.

And God continues to show up, proving the need to serve. This week, a young mother with five babies was sent my way. They had been homeless for three months. Her little boy had been bitten by a recluse spider, and his arm looked terrible. I was able to connect them with Catholic Charities, which helped with the deposit on a home. We got them moved in, secured furniture, pillows, and blankets, and several friends—along with local churches—stepped in to help.

It was just one more family that God put in my path, reminding me why I am here, why this mission matters, and why saving the shelter is so important.

I think of Nehemiah, who faced opposition while rebuilding Jerusalem's walls. His enemies ridiculed and threatened him, yet he prayed, stayed the course, and completed the work.

Like Nehemiah, I will keep my eyes on the mission. The shelter is meant to serve, and God will provide the means to keep it open. I trust Him.

Nehemiah 2:20

"The God of heaven will give us success. We, his servants, will start rebuilding, but as for you, you have no share in Jerusalem or any claim or historic right to it."

Count Your Blessings, One by One

Wow—what a week it has been! I am tired but deeply thankful. God has been moving in powerful ways through Embrace Hope, C Carter Crane, and I am so grateful to witness His hand at work. I share this as it is a reminder for us to pause, share God's blessings, large and small.

On Friday, we welcomed a new tenant into the shelter—a blessing for them and a reminder for all of us that everyone deserves a safe place to regroup. Monday brought even more joy as we helped a young man transition into low-income housing, opening the door to a fresh start and renewed hope.

Tuesday and Wednesday, through the generosity of Darby's Furniture and our Second Chance Clothes Closet, we were able to assist four flood victims with much-needed furnishings and clothing.

Thursday was a whirlwind: a referral came in for a woman struggling with addiction, and by God's grace, we connected her to a local drug and alcohol recovery program, Catalyst, where she will receive the specialized care she needs. The staff at Catalyst are amazing in helping with this—and I know in my heart, it will be okay.

Lawton First Assembly (LFA) continued to pour out blessings by providing beds—their faith in action is a beautiful testimony. That same day, we were called to help a veteran in crisis. By 3:00 p.m., he had toured homes, signed a lease, and secured stable housing. No veteran should face homelessness when so many stand ready to help—and I'm thankful we could be part of that story.

Late Thursday, after a long day, we received an unexpected donation of noodles, peanut butter, and pantry staples—a sweet reminder that even small gifts make a big difference.

Perhaps the most tender answered prayer came for the woman battling cancer and homelessness. She was brought back to Comanche County Memorial Hospital, where the nursing staff provided excellent care, and she agreed to enter Hospice. My prayer has been, "Lord, grant her grace and dignity," and He answered beyond measure. God is so good!

And the blessings keep coming—a friend is even bringing over Billy Sims Barbeque to the shelter!

How good is our community? So good. I love seeing Christ at work through His people.

Friends, count your blessings one by one. In the

middle of long days, unexpected challenges, and heart-heavy moments, God's love shines through in mighty and gentle ways. All praise goes to Him—He is our Provider. Never doubt.

Psalm 107:1

"Give thanks to the Lord, for He is good; His love endures forever."

Tailor-Made Grace

Yesterday, the owner and I were out checking on their rental properties. It's been a busy season, helping several individuals impacted by the recent flooding get moved or settled with their immediate needs.

As we worked, one young man involved in ministry shared that many of his suits had been ruined in the flood. Without missing a beat, I told him, "Come with me. Let's go to the Clothes Closet."

You see, just a few weeks ago, Lisa had cleaned out her husband's closet and generously donated several beautifully dry-cleaned suits to the shelter.

When the young man tried them on, something remarkable happened—they fit like they were tailor-made. The chest, the waist, the sleeves, the pant length—every detail a perfect match.

That's not coincidence. That's God. That's the heart of this community.

He sees. He knows. He provides.

In moments like this, I'm reminded how blessed we are to be part of God's work—one suit, one need, one life at a time, right here in Lawton, Oklahoma.

So, share the goodness. Celebrate it. I see it daily— our God is an awesome God!

Philippians 4:19

"And my God will supply every need of yours according to his riches in glory in Christ Jesus."

Today Was a Day of Much Reflection

I found myself thinking about the recent flooding and the heartbreak it's left behind. So many lives disrupted, homes destroyed, hearts broken. And I can't help but ask—how do we make sense of tragedy like this? Why do things like this happen?

The truth is, many of us wrestle with the sadness in this world. I know I do. Sometimes it's just too much to absorb, too much to process. We see devastation, loss, and heartache… and we feel helpless.

Yet, in the middle of all the sorrow, we catch a glimpse of hope. A young man battling cancer—the tumor on his spine has shrunk. The chemo is working. Prayers are being answered.

Even as others face unimaginable pain, we hold on to these moments of mercy. We celebrate the wins, while mourning the losses.

I don't have all the answers. I don't have the perfect words. But I do have faith. I believe in Christ. I believe in His promises—that even in a broken world, He is present. And that one day, He will make all things right. When the days are hard, when our hearts are broken, hit your knees. As for me, I'll be reminded to hit mine. Again and again.

Until the day the Lord reveals His promises, I will continue to trust, continue to pray, and continue to love through the hurt.

> **Revelation 21:4**
>
> "He will wipe every tear from their eyes. There will be no more death or mourning or crying or pain, for the old order of things has passed away."

"Stepping Out on Faith: God's Provision for the Shelter"

I want to close by sharing a testimony of how God has worked in my life—not only to transform me, but to reach countless others through the mission of providing shelter to those in need.

It was December 31, 2023. I was sitting at my desk, working on my dissertation on preventing homelessness among veterans, when the phone rang around 8:30 p.m. It was the local police. They were with a pregnant woman and six children, sitting homeless on the edge of the street, and they asked if I knew of any open shelters.

I called my son, and we went to help. That family was placed in an apartment. But afterward, I called the C Carter Crane shelter to check on their status—only to learn they were closed due to plumbing issues and would remain closed until the end of February. Worse yet, the woman on the phone said the shelter was closing permanently.

I was stunned. How could we not have a shelter? I called the board over the shelter. They had reached out to several agencies, but no one was willing to keep it open.

So I did what I knew to do—I prayed.

James 1:5 tells us, "If any of you lacks wisdom, let him ask of God, who gives to all liberally and without reproach, and it will be given to him."

I sought counsel from friends, including Burl, who said, "We need to try to keep the shelter open." Around the same time, Annie Grey approached me and said she had been praying for me to take the shelter on.

I went back to the board and told them, "If no one else will step up, I will."

Months passed, and on July 15, 2024, I woke up crying. Burl asked me what was wrong, and I said, "Today's the day the shelter is supposed to close." I confessed my frustration that I had prayed and prayed, but no one had come forward. Burl looked at me and said, "God gave you the answer. Step out on faith and take over the shelter. He will provide."

Proverbs 3:5-6 says, "Trust in the Lord with all your heart, and lean not on your own understanding; in all your ways acknowledge Him, and He shall direct your paths."

So I prayed again: "God, if this is the mission You have for me, make it clear." I promised, "I won't be like Jonah—I don't want three days in the belly of a whale. Show me the way."

I took the keys.

The shelter was in rough shape. It's an old WWII building with poor maintenance. I had a retired fire department inspector walk through and tell me what the critical fixes were. I switched over the utilities, and soon the bills started rolling in: an $900 electric bill, a $3,200 security system.

One day, as I sat at my desk crying and praying, a young woman named Kat appeared in my doorway. She handed me a check to help with the shelter. I thanked her and set it aside. Later, when I opened it, I saw the amount—$3,200.

At that moment, I said, "Lord, I will not question again that You have called me to this mission."

Philippians 4:19 says, "And my God will supply all your needs according to His riches in glory in Christ Jesus."

We put out a call for volunteers—167 people showed up to clean, repair, and organize the shelter. God kept sending help.

During this journey with the shelter, I reflected on

a night I was looking for my graduate thesis. While sorting through old papers, I came across my bucket list. I wept when I saw the materialistic desires of my younger self—I had on my list a Lincoln, a fur coat, trips, promotions, and my graduate degree. I started checking off the things I had accomplished, and I cried as I asked God to forgive me for my materialistic heart. That same night, I was blessed with five fur coats. A friend's mom passed, and the coats did not fit her. They fit me perfectly.

> Psalm 37:4 tells us, "Delight yourself in the Lord, and He will give you the desires of your heart."

I have seen God's hand over and over in my life to include recently:

While helping a young man affected by a flood, he shared how sad he was at the loss of his ministry suits. Because a young lady had cleaned out her husband's closet weeks earlier, we had suits that fit him like they were tailor-made at the shelter's clothes closet.

A church called about liquid nutrient drinks for feeding tubes. I shared I did not need them, but I could store them. The next day, a young man—battling cancer and on a feeding tube—arrived at the shelter. We had exactly what he needed.

Stepping Out on Faith

As I considered how to sustain the shelter long-term, God laid an idea on my heart. We have over 100 churches in our community. If each one gave $1,000 a year, alongside my own $14,000 contribution, we could meet our $114,000 annual budget. We called it the Faith Challenge. Our first year, we received 120 pledges. Churches bring food, clothes, and help with Thanksgiving, Christmas, and Easter.

> 2 Corinthians 9:8 promises, "And God is able to bless you abundantly, so that in all things at all times, having all that you need, you will abound in every good work."

Friends, I can tell you with all certainty, God is faithful.

He is Jehovah Jireh—the Lord who provides.

My encouragement to you is simple: If God calls you to a mission, trust Him. He will equip you. He will surround you with helpers. He will open the storehouses of heaven.

> Galatians 6:9 says, "Let us not grow weary while doing good, for in due season we shall reap if we do not lose heart."

Let's be the hands and feet of Christ. Let's step out in faith, knowing that where God guides, He provides.

Acknowledgements

Family, friends, and strangers we meet along our journey add value to our lives, and certainly mine. Thank you for allowing me to see Christ in our interactions, thank you for blessing me with your presence.